Printed in the United States of America

First Printing, 2020

Illustration: by Robby Wilburn

ISBN: 978-0-578-72133-0

Editor: Kyndal Gordon

This book is dedicated to my sweet
daughter Zaria, who has a smile that can
brighten up any day.
Baby girl, never lose your joy to smile.
Mommy loves you endlessly Zaria.

Mommy loves my smile.
She thinks it's great, so every morning I give her a big cheesseee, and then she kisses my face.

Mommy loves my smile.
It brings her joy. Every time she sees my smile, she tells me I'm the prettiest one in the world.

Mommy loves my smile.
She tells me this everyday, and it
makes me want to smile even more
to ensure / brighten up her day.

Mommy loves my smile.
It is definitely true, because even when mommy is sad, it can brighten up her blues.

Mommy loves my smile.
She never wants it to fade. She tells me no matter what anyone says, or does, to ensure you remember to smile every day.

5

Mommy loves my smile. She thinks it's unique. That makes me smile even harder from cheek to cheek.

Mommy loves my smile.
She says it just melts her heart.
I believe that is the best part
because mommy is the one who holds
the biggest place in my heart.

BUT WAIT !!!!
If you are
reading this, there is
one more thing....

If you smile at your mommy, I am sure she will think the same thing.

This book was written, not only as a dedication to my daughter, but also to remind all the moms, dads, and caretakers of children to show your children love every day. Encourage them to smile and to create happy moments that will make them smile just from the memory of them. Having the pure joy in your heart to smile daily is so important in this world today; but as moms, dads and caretakers of our children, it is our responsibility to protect and plant the seed of happiness and joy into our children. They will carry this happiness and joy with them and pass it along to others.

Thank you so much for reading
Mommy Loves My Smile.